The Will of My Father.
A WestsWords Publication
Copyright © 2008
ISBN: 9780615213286
WestsWords Publishing
Columbus, Ohio
All rights reserved. No part of this book may be reproduced in any form electronically or mechanically without the written permission of publisher except for reviewer purposes.
Published by WestsWords Publishing
First Edition

THE WILL OF MY FATHER

MINISTER YOLANDA WEST

POEMS AND PROSE OF PRAISE

WestsWords
COLUMBUS, OHIO

**TO MY PARENTS VERSIA AND ANNIE WEST
FOR THEIR LOVE, GUIDANCE, STRONG FAITH AND FOR HELPING ME FIND THE LORD.**

Table of Contents

The Will of My Father 3
Inheritance 4
Do It In the Name of Jesus 5
Love 6
Let's Break it Down 7
Blood Bought 8
Right and Holy 9
In Vain 10
Blame Game 11
Armed and Dangerous 12
Rock and Roll 13
Cookie Jar 14
Happy Birthday Jesus 15
Shape, Make and Mold 16
Intelligent Demons 17
The Eternal Story 18
Self-Rising 19
Life 20
A Man That Loves the Lord 21
It's Time for Saints 22
Give Me Flowers 23
Willing and Able 24
For Dad 26
Best Friend 27
These Eyes 28
God Made 29
Use Me Lord 30
Grace 31
Tick Tock 32
God in Action 33
Homegoing 34

Every Road Has to End	35
Stick Up	36
Christian Alphabet	37
Power and Authority	39
Judgment	40
Keep It Simple	42
Lose Out	43
Jesus the Star	44
A Praying Grandmother	45
Keep Your Eyes on Jesus	46
Tell Jesus	47
The Things Mary Pondered	48
Kept	49
Jesus for Mine	50
Backsliding Children	51
A Mother Does the Best She Can	53
About the Author	55

The Will of My Father

Before I knew what Christ was about

When things did not go my way

I used to get mad, pout

knocking my head against the wall

crying at times and wondering "Why?"

But as time went on, I found out, by and by

It was not about me

It was the will of my Father you see.

I found out my soul wasn't my own,

I was bought and paid for with the blood of Jesus

It was not about me,

I came to do the will of my Father you see.

Inheritance

My Father is a King

He owns the earth and her fullness

I have rights

Because I live for Jesus Christ

If I have a need

He will supply it

Whatever my Father wants I say "I can".

I don't worry because He owns the land

And when He went to Calvary

He left me eternal life and all his promises

Won't you join in our family?

Let Jesus help you be all He wants you to be

Don't you want your inheritance?

Let GOD give you that chance

He is the only one who can.

The Will of My Father

Do It In the Name of Jesus

Oh, how precious is the name of Jesus

Oh, how precious is the name of Jesus

O, if we could see

Let's stop and think

A man that died upon Calvary for you and me

The Will of My Father

Love

I know what it is

I know what it is not

Who has it to give?

And who has not

It is not just what you say

It's what you do that reflects the true you

GOD so loved the world He gave his only begotten son.

There is a word there

I'm looking for.

Did you discover it? GAVE

He gave his begotten son

GAVE is a action word

He didn't simply talk about giving; He did it.

That's our example of love.

Let's Break it Down

Men this one's for you:

God created you in his image.

He wouldn't treat women the way some of you do.

He said love your wife, as He loves the church.

That is what He meant.

He doesn't care what man is doing or saying

God's word will stand.

God has a perfect plan.

The Will of My Father 8

Blood Bought

We all can confess with our mouths

and believe in our hearts that Jesus Christ is LORD

but can we all say we've been

Redeemed in the name of Jesus?

Or are we trying to convince someone else to believe us?

I don't know about you but I've been Blood Brought

I will take up my cup of salvation and call upon the name of the Lord

As I travel this journey.

I've found it isn't hard

the blood that paid for me was the blood of Jesus you see.

Oh what a wonderful change in me.

What a wonderful savior is He?

Oh praise His name

Jesus Christ what a gain.

Thank you for purchasing me way back on cavalry

I am Blood bought you see.

Right and Holy

Because a thing is right

Does not mean it is holy

We need more of God's people, to stand and say this boldly.

Because something is right before our eyes,

does not make it holy.

Everything is not by our sight.

We can think we are right but,

if it's not according to the word of God,

it's not right.

Holy is right and is by the Word

You can stand up and say "It is so, thus sayith the Lord."

Go by My word. It isn't hard.

The Will of My Father

In Vain

Lord, they take your name in vain

They don't understand

They believe that a blessing is what you have.   I know it is what you don't have.

They talk about things they don't even know

They say your name but they don't take your direction.

They sing in vain.

They teach and preach in vain.

They know of your name they don't know you.

I pray they would love you as I do.

The Will of My Father

Blame Game

Everyone blames something or someone else.

Very seldom do we take the blame for ourselves

Admitting when we are wrong

Suffering the consequences can be good

I believe the situation can be understood.

Trying to place blame everywhere

it just doesn't belong.

What a song it would be to sing a sad sad song,

don't be a part of the blame game.

Learn from your mistakes and make a change.

Standing up for what's right and rejecting all that is wrong

Looking forward to one day being in my heavenly home

Stop the blame game and stand up for His name

Armed and Dangerous

A Christian that lives by God's word

Is a person to be heard?

They are armed and dangerous

bold and victorious

They not only listen to the word

These Christians live it

The enemy is on the outlook for these the most

But an armed and dangerous child of god can put an end to fight by calling

on the Lord.

They just don't wait until trouble comes

They call on Him day by day

one by one

The enemy knows who they are and so does the Lord

Satan doesn't approach them in any way

he has to be careful about what he does and say.

They are armed, dangerous, and notorious

Get armed and dangerous in your life

Rock and Roll

I once heard a singer that was told he should be singing rock and roll.

He said his feet were on a rock and his name was on a roll.

I thought to myself, "What a way to go?"

I bet you thought I was talking about something else.

Those who know will say she is not herself.

Sometimes we can take one line and put things out of their place and time.

So when you hear rock and roll think twice before you assume what's going to be told.

The Will of My Father

Cookie Jar

Don't be like the kid caught with his hand in the cookie jar.

Caught in the act

No sin will pass when Jesus comes back

Taking the cookies without permission seems too sweet.

But with actions like that the devil you will meet

It may seem like the wrong way is the best way at times.

No sins will pass, not even one lie

Get your hand out of the cookie jar.

Straight is the only way.

Who wants to be caught in the cookie jar?

Not me

Amen

The Will of My Father

Happy Birthday Jesus

Happy Birthday, Jesus

Thank you for going to Calvary many centuries ago

to claim our souls,

That we could be free from sin

To have the right to be born again

All because of your love for the world

You don't discriminate against any man, woman, boy or girl

Love by example is the powerful tool you left for us to use

You are the reason for the season

Not Santa gifts or toys

Your birth has brought joy to all saints, believers, and Christians in this

world

Happy Birthday, Jesus

You are truly the reason

The Will of My Father

Shape, Make and Mold

In our eyes, we see ourselves as the best thing in sight

In God's eyes He has to break us down

before we are fit for His sight

He takes off this and puts on that.

When He gets through we're fit for the kingdom and that's a fact

Lying can't go

Coveting, oh no

Busy bodying

Or any unrighteous thing

no sin will go before our Lord and Savior

He has to shape make and mold us

This is not questioned but is a must

If we want to see His face, we all have to be shaped, made and molded.

Intelligent Demons

There are all kinds of people

Smart, dumb, lunatics and intelligent

Intelligent people think they can't be possessed

Demons use people like God does.

Don't be ignorant of his device or he will use them on you

People judge people by their outer appearance

But God's people look at your spirit

People all dress in suits and ties

The inside doesn't match the outer facade

They can possess anyone who allows it and especially those with no

power.

The Will of My Father

The Eternal Story

Everyone has heard of the street paved with gold.

But there is a story that hasn't been told

Eternal is eternity.

Life is never ending

Never to see darkness again

a life without sin

It's not the world we are in today

Talking and acting like everything's okay

It's the everlasting peace, joy and rest

All of our life's eternal happiness

Serving God

He chose us from the rest

The other's settled for less

Honestly, we really don't know

It's an eternal story that must be seen and not just told

That's the only way you can know

Come on, don't you want to go?

The Will of My Father

Self-Rising

Some of us think we're enriched like flour

An ingredient to be used

Our awakening comes from

The same One who made the skies

Some think they woke themselves up

Actually it is because of God you breathe and speak?

Man thinks he can do anything

But we are limited human beings

Self-rising -you can think

that with belief you surely will sink

Life

Life is what you make it

I've heard that so many times

Here's a theory of mine

Trials and errors we all make

But the key is to learn from our mistakes.

To know which bumps and curves

Never to experience again

makes each and every one of us

better women and men.

Sometimes we make mistakes more than twice

But with the help of our Lord it's not all of our life

It took most of my years to find

out how precious and dear life is to me

I want to live unbound.

I'm going to live life free

I found out just what life means to me.

The Will of My Father

A Man That Loves the Lord

It doesn't matter how he looks.

Or if he's built and all hooked

It matters if he loves God,

when he's got it from above.

It doesn't matter what he has or has not.

When he has Jesus, I will tell you what he's got

He's has it all.

It's nothing like a man who responds to God's call

It doesn't matter if he's tall dark and handsome

As long as he loves the One who paid

the price with his life for our ransom.

If a man loves God

He can love you.

The Will of My Father

It's Time for Saints

It's time for the Saints to be the Saints.

The Aints to be the Aints

Whose side are you on?

You cannot serve two masters.

It's either God or man.

There is no in between.

There is either heaven or hell.

It's your choice.

Choose well

Give Me Flowers

Give me my flowers while I yet live

Not just the roses, tulips or sunflowers

But an encouraging word, a heavenly smile or a prayer

If I've done something, right

It might make things a little brighter

Why do we wait until our love ones are gone

to sing them a praise song?

Do and say while they are with you.

Don't forget to tell them you love them too

Give me my flowers while I yet live

Tell me some things while I can hear,

instead of waiting and withholding because of fear.

Give me my flowers while I'm still here.

The Will of My Father

Willing and Able

I know you've heard about

Cain and Able

But do you know about willing and able?

We are children of God, we are supposed to be willing and know that God

is able.

Stop depending on self.

Know that, it is Jesus.

He doesn't need help.

Only then are you willing and understand He is able

You can't lose.

Even people in Christ, try to plan their lives.

Sorry you are no longer your own

Are you willing?

Because He is able.

My Lord

Drugs can be a lord

Alcohol can be a lord

You need to know your lord

Whatever you put before God is your lord

That means anything.

Let me tell you about my Lord - He is the King of Kings

He can do anything

My Lord will be with you when you're down and out

My Lord will give you a reason to shout

My Lord will show you what real living is all about

The Will of My Father

For Dad

For all the things

I didn't get to say

I love you Dad and I miss you even today.

You went away before I could tell you

Dad, I am the happiest I've ever been in my life

Since I came to know Jesus Christ

You know Dad, I have to admit, it gets hard

But I know my true Lord

I wish you could see the life I'm living

Learning, sharing and giving.

I wish I could have made you happy

Before you passed away but

The thought of you came to me in a conversation today.

I love you Dad always

This one is for you Dad.

Best Friend

Let me tell you about my best friend

He's the kind of friend who will love you to the end

People let me tell you about my best friend

He will stick with you through thick and thin

People let me tell you how He brought me out

Took me out of sin and taught me what He's all about

My best friend name is Jesus Christ

Would you like to invite Him into you life?

The Will of My Father

These Eyes

There was a song out years ago when I was young

As I recall it was by Jr. Walker

These eyes have seen many things

Many tears have clung to my face

But thank God for His grace

Now I have seen the glory of the Lord

I carry His glory in my eyes this day forward.

It's not a joke to Satan he can't stand the sight,

of me winning my battle, my fight.

So now after many years of so much pain

I thank God once again for using my pain for His gain.

The Will of My Father

God Made

God made the world with all kinds of people

Short, tall, big and small

With all different types of personalities

God made us all

Wouldn't it be boring if we were all the same?

It's nice not to know what's to be thrown in the game.

The game of life can be exciting and nice.

I saw this man singing today.

I thought to myself that he is always that way.

Each time I see him, he sings so loud

I thought if I could be like that for Jesus. He would be so proud

That man inspired me to think about the types of people God made,

and about God's amazing grace.

We are all different that's for sure.

Some so rude and harsh while others are so pure,

Have you ever wondered why some people were made a certain way?

Or do you think it's an accident we are not the same?

We're all made God's way

by His grace, in His image and His name

We are God made

The Will of My Father

Use Me Lord

Some people say I'm too nice.

Some say I'm too good.

But I tell Jesus to use me if he would.

So many have used me in other ways

I didn't mind.

Use me Jesus use me all the time.

They say everything must come to an end.

Use me Jesus, my best friend.

Until you take away my breath.

Jesus until there's nothing of me left.

It can't be harder than the road

I've traveled.

If it is Lord, You will be the example I follow to Calvary.

Grace

Saving Grace

Keeping Grace

It has to be done with faith

Grace that He will save you and keep you.

and all the other thing's He will do.

Just the faith of a mustard seed.

That's all you need.

Stand on God's words and take heed.

Tick Tock

Tick Tock goes the clock.

Time is running out.

I bet you're wondering what this is all about

Well as the story goes

There is a Heaven or hell for sure.

One day the clouds are going to crack.

Within an instant, Jesus will be back.

Tick Tock goes the clock.

Are you ready to meet Jesus Christ, The Rock?

If not time is running out.

God in Action

GOD is love

He gave His life, a living sacrifice

We that are His followers

Need to live by His motto

Love one another not only just our sisters and brothers

Love is not only to say "I love you."

Put actions with your words

Not just speaking to be heard

Have you ever heard someone who is all talk?

Well GOD is action

And He will use me and you.

Homegoing

When you hear of my passing away don't weep for me.

I'm just going home to be with JESUS you see

In my Father's house are many mansions if was not true He wouldn't have told me.

It's now my time to go.

You may miss me and it is ok,

but I was looking forward to this day.

My body has to go but not my soul

Read God's word it will tell you what you need to know

I don't want you all sadden with tears

Think about all my struggles over the years

Now that it is all over for me

Thank you Jesus for coming for me,

It's my home going rejoice and be glad.

The devil is mad about this soul he couldn't have.

Take your place in church today.

The Lord wants it that way.

There could be a soul saved today.

Every Road Has to End

Have you ever seen a road that does not end?

I tell you we can go through some things

It seems like it is never going to be over

I was talking to this mother and she said, "Darling, every road has to end.

But some of you might have to travel it again."

I pray to God never to put this trail in my life again.

The Will of My Father

Stick Up

Turn around raise your hands don't look at me look up to the Man.

Start praising for your life

It's you on the line not your children or wife

Hallelujah is the highest praise you can give

Start now if you want to continue to live

Put some "Thank You, Jesus!" in there too

This is my hold up you'll do what

I want you to do

While I have your attention

It's about his death, burial and resurrection.

Christian Alphabet

Although things aren't perfect

Because of trials or pain

Continue in thanksgiving

Do not began to blame

Even when the times are hard

Fierce winds are bound to blow

God is forever able

Hold on to what you know

Imagine life without His love

Joy would cease to be

Keep thanking Him for all things

Love imparts to thee

Move out of camp complaining

No weapon

On earth can wield the power

Praise can do it alone

The Will of My Father

Quit looking at the future

Redeem the time at hand

Start everyday with worship

To thank God is a command

Until we see Him coming

Victorious in the sky

We'll run the race with gratitude

EXalting God most high

Yes, there will be good times and bad

Zion waits with a glory where no one is sad

The Will of My Father

Power and Authority

Power and authority is not pride

Power and authority comes from up high.

Power and authority is not rude and cold.

Power and authority is just being plain bold

Power and authority doesn't come from people

Power and authority comes from Jesus

Power and authority is not an age

It's whom ever Jesus says makes the grade.

Power and authority or pride

This is your choice out of life

Power and authority it knows no boundaries

Would you like to find it?

Judgment

We Live

We Die

Then comes judgment

Damnation or eternal Life

We are all going to stand before Jesus Christ

Man, woman, boy or girl

Judgment will come for everyone in the world

Pay attention to God's word it will be fulfilled

You have a chance now to do God's will

Don't wait until that day

Thinking everything is okay

You may have a rude awakening on Judgment Day

Get your house in order

The Will of My Father

Get baptized in His cooling water

Get reborn and get rid of your sin

Get ready for judgment

Because that day it will come.

Read your bible to see what else will be done

Surely His kingdom will come.

Keep It Simple

Keep it simple

Make it plain

Teach My people

About My name

Feed My sheep

So they won't be weak

Feed My flock

Prove to them I'm their rock

Tell them once they have learned about My name

Their lives will never be the same

Jesus Christ is My name

Salvation is My game

Tell it so they'll understand

Just keep it simple and make it plain

The Will of My Father

Lose Out

As I watch people passing looking through my booth

Some walking, some smoking

I thought about Heaven

There wouldn't be any smoking there

That is a place with no cares

Lose out

We lose out because of our habits

and how we live our lives.

Some of us are going to miss Jesus Christ

We want to do things our way

But it is going to be my Jesus who says "I'm giving you time before judgment comes."

My will be done

No excuse will I hear

I've been warning far and near

I love you can't you see

If I didn't I would be warning you of what is to be.

Don't lose out on Me

Jesus the Star

He didn't come for fame

Only to save

He didn't come to make a name for Himself

Saving souls is His game

People run to the movie stars

Mention Jesus name and they run

Football, baseball stadiums are filled

People don't want to come to church and do God's will

The enemies have people so blind

They run from the One who can save their behinds

People recognize the stars in the sky

But not the star for the One who died for us

So that our souls could be, free

Many stars come out at night

But there is only one Star that lived, died and had to rise again

That star is Jesus Christ.

A Praying Grandmother

To all the praying Grandmothers, just a few words of encouragement to say

Even in the times that we are living in

Keep praying but not just for your kin

Pray for others as if you are praying for yourself.

Let's get prayers through for someone else

While we are crying out for God

He is working out our problems that seem so hard.

There is something about a grandmother, who prays,

Her wisdom, knowledge and caring ways

Just going through things in her days makes her so grand

In her grandchildren's eyes, she is their greatest fan

So keep praying grandmothers even for the ones you don't know

While you're praying there is still hope

Keep Your Eyes on Jesus

Keep our eyes on Jesus

If you take them off you may be led astray

Glue them to Jesus and let them stay

I know that you can get distracted

Don't linger on the things you see

Jesus says keep your eyes on me.

I know it might be hard when someone is doing you wrong

Find a way somehow with a melody of a song

Just keep your eyes on Jesus

Let Him show you the way

God keeps His promises and He promised a better day.

Tell Jesus

One day all of life's struggles were taking a toll

I use to try to express them to someone on the phone

I soon found it wasn't getting me anywhere

As I thought about it, there was only One who I knew truly cared

So as I lay in my bed praying I began to pour out my heart

I wanted to tell someone but I heard a voice say. "Tell it to the Lord."

I got up to write down what the voice said

"Tell Jesus." It kept ringing in my head.

Whatever you feel need to be discussed

Tell Jesus if your heart is full of pain

Man cannot do anything about

Oh praise His name - tell Jesus

When there have been losses instead of gain

Whatever life brings you, tell Jesus

He'll always know. Just tell Jesus.

The Things Mary Pondered

Can you imagine God sending you a message?

to carry and raise his son?

Imagine what Mary thought when God asked this of her.

She could have become proud and boastful

But she remained humble and was lead by God's word instead

I don't know if I could have been as humble as Mary

Even though it was an honor I know I couldn't have filled Mary's shoes

If she really wanted to talk about it

There would have been no one who could understand

Not even her cousin Elizabeth whose child was of a man

When God chooses you sometimes the job won't be an easy job to do

When he chooses the job it is meant just for you

Thank You Mary for being our savior

I know all the things you must have pondered in your heart

About your son, our Savior and our Lord

I can only imagine it was hard

But her mission was accomplished with the birth of our Lord

Kept

Kept from death

Kept from losing my mind

Kept from doing time

Kept from traps

Kept because I was here for something else

Kept for the journey He had in store for me

Kept from the bottomless pit.

Introduce yourself to your neighbor

Use your first name, of course, but your middle name should be "Kept."

The Will of My Father

Jesus for Mine

Some take alcohol

Some even take drugs

I take to Jesus and get high of His love from above

Some are hooked on coffee

Some even hooked on tea

But for me it's Jesus you see

Some people are soda pop drinkers

Still it's Jesus for me

Some love money

Some are hooked on lovers

I'll take Jesus for mine

Some are hooked on doing wrong

But I tell you I'm hooked on gospel song

for some of those things there was a time

But now I tell you I'll take Jesus for mine

The Will of My Father

Backsliding Children

Sometimes we look over our loves

Thinking about the wrong, and what

we could have done to make them right

Things in life have always been hard for me.

I ask the Lord for my children not to let it be.

There were two things I asked the Lord and He heard me.

That all my children finish school and learn to drive.

He heard me as I prayed.

Now I ask for the most important thing.

Help them find their way back to Jesus Christ.

Growing up, I gave them to You, Lord

but they turned their back.

What could I do?

But never stop praying and hoping and waiting.

That He reclaim backsliding children.

Not just mine but all.

Show them which way to go.

The Will of My Father

This is a prayer that all saved parents pray.

They pray for help.

They pray that they come back before it's too late.

He will bring them back.

It may take a while.

For every backsliding child I pray.

Bring them home Jesus,

I know You hear us when we pray.

The Will of My Father

A Mother Does the Best She Can

How do you know that you've done your best?

It's when you've taught your children about Jesus.

He will do the rest.

How could you expect something from your children,

that you do not do?

They are looking up to you.

Don't you know if we start being an example?

they will follow.

We should be proud of our children of tomorrow.

Some people think it is all about the fad.

I see it as being really sad.

Children are learning some things that they

don't need to know.

They need more parents to show them which way to go.

They are being taught worldly things

But do they know about Jesus Christ?

The Will of My Father

He is the real King of Kings.

Your kids may wear the best

Does this make them better than all the rest?

Just because our kids may be street smart,

Doesn't mean they don't need the Lord in their heart.

Think about what I'm saying

People we need to get down with some praying.

I'm just trying to say

We need the Lord to make it today.

If you've brought Jesus into their lives

You know you've done right.

Continue to pray.

Jesus, we surrender to You.

About the Author

Minister Yolanda West found Jesus at an early age. It wasn't long before she realized her true calling was to teach the word of God.

www.ingramcontent.com/pod-product-compliance
Lightning Source LLC
Chambersburg PA
CBHW051717040426
42446CB00008B/924